Formosa's Masquerade

written and illustrated by

Ying Syuan Huang

Archway Publishing books may be ordered through booksellers or by contacting:

Archway Publishing
1663 Liberty Drive
Bloomington, IN 47403
www.archwaypublishing.com
1-(888)-242-5904

ISBN: 978-1-4808-0971-0 (sc)
ISBN: 978-1-4808-0970-3 (e)

Printed in the United States of America.

Archway Publishing rev. date: 2/11/2015

Dedication

For Austin and his mother.

Preface

This children's book could help parents, teachers, or educators engage conversations, encourage imaginations, and create more stories with their children. This book is especially for parents who are interested in Taiwanese culture or want their children to explore diverse cultures. It is also practical for teachers and educators who want to introduce a fun story that they could expand on for students' learning and classroom discussions. In this book, there are many cultural elements waiting for you and your children to discover. Enjoy!

Acknowledgement

This children's book was funded by the National Science Council in Taiwan. I would like to especially thank to Xuan-ting Lin, who has helped me with the illustrations and graphic designs of this book. would like to thank Professor Su-hui Lin for being mentoring and supervising this project. She has always encouraged me to pursue my ideas and express them freely by drawing and creating, and this has helped me realize dreams I thought were impossible. Also, I have to thank all my friends in Taiwan who stood by me and helped me complete this book. Thank you for falling into the world of a storybook and enjoying the adventure with me.

Introduction

Formosa is a young boy who loves reading storybooks and has always dreamed of becoming one of the characters in the stories. Every night around bedtime, Formosa is happy and looks forward to seeing his friends in the storybooks. Little does Formosa know that he is about to embark on an exciting adventure and unexpected challenges in the world of his favorite storybooks.

Formosa fell asleep with a smile after reading his favorite storybook. This peaceful rest did not last long as he began to fall deeper and deeper into the abyss. When Formosa was able to gather himself after a scary descend, he quickly found himself in a place that looks identical to one that is portrayed in his favorite storybook. Soon after Formosa lands, he began to encounter all the characters he has ever drawn on in the storybook. These angry characters demand justice from Formosa. Is this a dream? Will Formosa be able to overcome this adversity and make friends? How will Formosa get out of this storybook world? Dive into the story right now and follow Formosa through his incredible journey!

Prologue

Hi! I am Formosa! I love reading storybooks just like you! But, remember not to draw all over your storybooks. Otherwise, you will fall into the story world like me!!! OOOOooooooooh~~~~ and I don't know how to get out of the story world~~~~~! Help!!!

"Close your story book! Time to sleep, Formosa", said Mommy.

As Formosa fell soundly asleep, he began to dream…
Formosa SUDDENLY fell off his bed and into the world of a storybook.

Formosa quickly noticed the curly mustache, piggy nose, and thick eyebrows on Mazu Goddess. Formosa burst out laughting.
Mazu Goddess said angrily, "You're a bad child! You drew all over my face, and I can only hide in my carriage now! How dare you laugh at me for what you have done!!! You are making me so angry!!!"

Suddenly, Formosa started to fall again.

Down to the ground Formosa fell.

The sound of firecrackers surrounded him as he gained consciousness.

bamBAMMbammmBAAAMMMM!!!

Formosa realized that it was the time of the Lunar New Year. He became very frightened because during the Lunar New Year, Monster Nian roamed around scaring children.

Suddenly, Monster Nian, who had a full-grown beard, started chasing Formosa, yelling. "Are you the Formosa who likes to scribble all over storybooks? You scribbled all over my body, and now my friends are laughing at me because I look funny."

Formosa remembered that he loves to draw all over storybooks. He realized what made Mazu Goddess and Monster Nian so upset.

"I'm so sorry," Formosa cried, "I'm so so sorry!!"

"I will never draw in storybooks again!" he said.

Formosa kept running to get away from Monster Nian's attack, and finally got rid of him.

But still, he had no way of getting out of the storybook. Feeling anxious, Formosa burst into tears.

An angel heard the sound of Formosa crying. The angel appeared before Formosa and mumbled, "Why are you crying, Formosa? Don't cry Formosa. Why are you crying, Formosa? Don't cry Formosa."

Formosa looked up at the angel and replied, "I upset Mazu Goddess because I drew all over the storybook. It made her look funny, so she's very upset with me."

"Cute little Formosa. Mazu Goddess is our goddess of the sea. She won't be upset with you as long as you say sorry to her," said the angel.

Formosa replied, "But, I don't know where to find Mazu Goddess! I want to get out of the storybook... I miss my Mommy!!!"

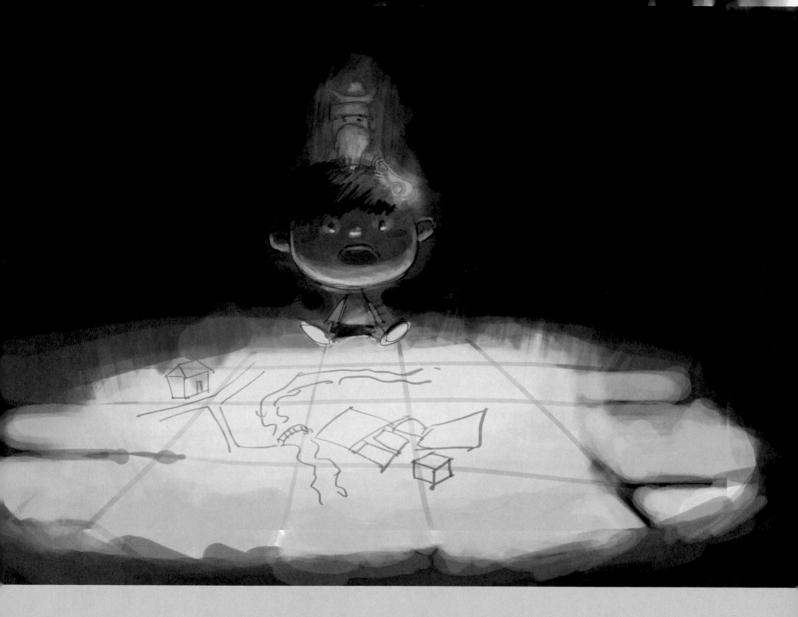

The angel gave Formosa a map he had seen in the storybook.
"Cute little Formosa. I can only offer you this map! I wish you good luck," the
angel said.
And with that, the angel disappeared.

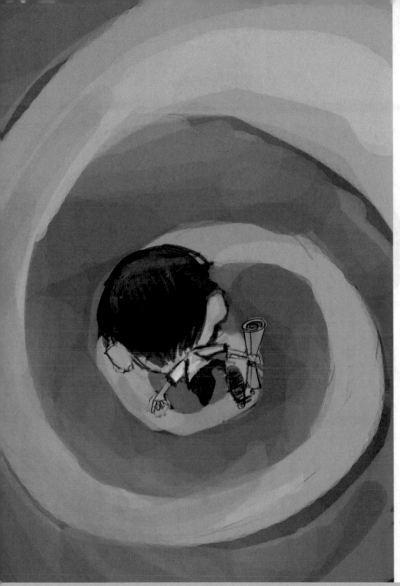

After the angel disappeared, Formosa fell into a magical spiral…
BAAAMMM!!!!! He fell to the floor of his room. But, he felt something was different…

Formosa walked out of his room and realized that he was in a flying house.
"This is so cooool!!!" he thought.
With excitement, Formosa stuck his head out of his flying house and realized
that there were many other flying houses beside his.

As he was looking out the window, Formosa realized he was tired and hungry. Suddenly, a big and tall candy house in the shape of Taipei 101 appeared before him! The candy house was so tall that Formosa could not see the top of the house! Formosa was ecstatic to see such a magnificent building.

Formosa's house collided with the candy house.

"GU RU GU RU." Formosa's house rolled down the mountain and made Formosa's world upside down, around and around.

Formosa was still tired and hungry, but he found himself in front of the candy house.
He started to bang on the door and hoped to have something sweet to eat.
"Knock! Knock! Knock!" "Knock! Knock! Knock!"
"Is anyone there? Is anyone home?"
Formosa was so hungry that he almost fainted.
He decided to take a bite of the doorknob, which was made of donut, hoping to
quiet the grumbling in his stomach.

"You glutton! How dare you eat my candy house behind my back! I have to punish you!," Auntie Tigress shouted!

Formosa was terrified!!! He remembered the rumor that Auntie Tigress likes to eat children's fingers!!!

Auntie Tigress said, "Since it's my birthday today, I will turn you into my birthday cake!", then she wiggled her tail as she turned Formosa into a huge birthday cake.

Auntie Tigress licked the cream on Formosa with her long and disgusting tongue, breathing horrible breath on Formosa. Her tongue was so long. It was terrifying! Auntie Tigress was so oily! It was so repulsive!

Auntie Tigress murmured as she stirred the pot, "I will turn you back into a delicious birthday cake and have you as a treat after I give you a shower!" Formosa knew that he had to find a way out, so he started to talk to Auntie Tigress. "Aunt Tigress, I am just a little Formosa now. I would make a tiny tiny cake if you were to eat me now! This would not be very satisfying!" he pleaded. "But today is my birthday! You are my birthday cake and I will eat you tonight!" Aunt Tigress said.

Formosa didn't give up. He said, "If I were to grow up to be big and round, that would make me even more delicious!"

After considering the, Auntie Tigress agreed with Formosa and said, "Short little thin Formosa, you are my birthday cake! I will turn you into a birthday cake next year. I will eat you on my birthday next year!"

"If I weren't here and now with you, how would you celebrate this birthday?" Formosa asked.

After much thinking, Aunt Tigress broke out in tears.

"No one is willing to celebrate my birthday and sing the birthday song to me because no one likes me," and she kept crying.

Formosa felt so sorry for her. He didn't know that Auntie Tigress was so lonely. Formosa started to wonder if Auntie Tigress wasn't as scary as the rumor he had heard. So, Formosa decided to give Auntie Tigress the birthday present he had received this year. As he took out a pacifier from his pocket and handed it to Auntie Tigress, he said, "I am sorry, Auntie Tigress. I should have asked you before eating your candy house. I hope you can forgive me. Please accept this pacifier as my birthday present to you! Happy Birthday, Auntie Tigress!"

Auntie Tigress burst happily into dance as she sucked on the pacifier. She said, "Mischievous Formosa, you are the first child who has ever given me a birthday present!!! Thank you!!!"

Auntie Tigress learned the joy of sharing from Formosa. For this reason, Auntie Tigress decided to share the candy house with everyone. Formosa also helped Auntie Tigress open her candy house to all the children. Since then, Auntie Tigress has made many great friends.

However, Formosa had to move to keep looking for Mazu Goodness so he could get out of the storybook. It was time to say goodbye to Auntie Tigress.

Formosa continued on his journey to find Mazu Goodness.

At night, Formosa lit up a flying lantern to help him look for his way home. He knew that his Mommy would be worrying about him if she couldn't find him. With every flying lantern that lit up, Formosa made a wish. A wish that he could go home soon.

All of a sudden, the flame of Formosa's flying lantern went out. Formosa found himself falling and stepping into nothingness...

    Down and down he went...

    Down and down he went...

    Falling endlessly...

Formosa started to think to himself, "Why did Mazu Goddess bring me into this storybook? Why? Why? Why?"

SPLASH!!!!!

Formosa fell into a river.

As he pulled his head out of the water, he saw countless dragon boats heading toward him in a battle ship formation!

"HELP~~~~~~~~~~~", he yelled.

No one could hear Formosa because of the beating drums on the dragon boats.

"HELP~~~~~~~~~~~", Formosa kept yelling.

He didn't know what to do.

Suddenly, a water ghost showed up to drag Formosa out of the dragon boat festival.

The water ghost took a good look at Formosa and said, "You're a little child, Formosa. You are supposed to be sleeping now. It is very dangerous for you to be playing around out here."

Formosa replied, "Thank you for pulling me out from the dragon boat festival. I am lost. I can't make my way home. Can you please help me?"

The water ghost said, "I can't! I can't! I can't help you! I am only a powerless water ghost and I work for the King of Hell here. I am told to do my job! I have to do my job!!!"

"What is it that you do?" Formosa asked.

"The life of a new Formosan salmon is supposed to take the place of yours. If I let you go, the King of Hell won't forgive me... but, you're just a kid, I can't have your life...I really don't know what to do." The water ghost started to panic.

Suddenly, the ground began to shake violently. It was a huge earthquake.
Big rocks on the surrounding mountains began to fall into water.
The water ghost was terrified.
All Formosan salmon were trying to find places to hide.

It was the anger of the King of Hell!!!!
The King of Hell suddenly appeared and yelled, "YOU DISAPPOINTING
WATER GHOST!!! HOW DARE YOU LET FORMOSA GO? I only gave you
just one job to do, but you couldn't even do it right. I have to punish you! You
will stay in a jail FOREVER!!!!!"

Formosa realized that the water ghost was now in trouble because of him. So, Formosa thought, "I have to stand up for the water ghost this time! I can't be afraid anymore. I have to save the water ghost."

Then, he shouted, "PLEASE LET THE WATER GHOST GO! HE DID NOT DO ANYTHING WRONG!!!"

Suddenly, Mazu Goddess appeared!!!

Mazu Goddess turned to Formosa and said, "Formosa! What you just did was very brave! You weren't afraid of the evil and you stood up for your friend. So, I am here to save you."

"BUT, don't be happy so soon, Formosa," Mazu Goddess said.

Formosa replied, "I am very sorry for scribbling in the storybook. Please help me get out of the storybook."

Mazu Goddess went on, "I made you fall into this storybook because I wanted you to go to the masquerade for me tomorrow. I don't want to embarrass myself in front of the public because you drew all over my face. You have to be responsible for what you did!!!!!"

Mazu Goddess disappeared again.

Formosa and the water ghost became good friends. The water ghost also gave Formosa his blessing, hoping that Formosa would be able to arrive at the masquerade in time.

In order to thank Formosa, the water ghost instructed the army of Formosan salmon to protect Formosa.
Formosa started on his way to attend the masquerade at Sun Moon Lake.

Although Formosa was exhilarated when he arrived at the gate of Sun Moon Lake, he still had no idea on what to wear for the masquerade.

Formosa appeared to be the only one who was not well prepared for the masquerade.

"What to wear"", he pondered.

As Formosa was worring about the masquerade, he heard some noises in the bamboo forest behind him.

Formosa realized that there were two people with their faces masked who were trying to catch a third person known as the Two-Tooth Man.
"Hey! What are your guys doing? Please stop!" Formosa shouted.

Formosa's shouting scared the two masked people and they quickly ran off. But, Two-Tooth Man burst into tears because they had stolen his bag of beans. "Without those beans, I can't keep my promise to spread happiness to every corner of the world", Two-Tooth Man said.

"I eat one bean a day in order to bring laughter and happiness to people every-where", he said.

"But now, I have lost the beans that were given to me by an old man. What can I do?"
Two-Tooth Man started to wail.

"Smile!!!! Two-Tooth Man!" Formosa tried to make Two-Tooth Man happy.
Formosa remembered how his mother taught him about making friends happy
when they are upset.

"Smile, and the world will smile back to you. This is what my Mommy says to
me whenever I am upset."

As Two-Tooth Man smiled, all the butterfly orchids he had made before could hear he crying. They all surrounded Two-Tooth Man and Formosa to cheer them up.

Filled with butterfly orchids, Formosa and Two-Tooth Man slowly transformed into butterflies.

They flew happily around the orchids.

Finally, Formosa showed up at the masquerade as an attractive butterfly.
Everyone watched Formosa with fascination as Formosa flew over Sun Moon Lake.
"Formosa! Formosa! Formosa!", the crowd cheered on!

Formosa was smiling while he was sleeping.
"He must be having a good, sweat, happy dream now," Formosa's Mommy thought.
Good night. Formosa!

Glossary

Auntie Tigress

Auntie Tigress, also known as a Tigress Witch, Hu Gu Po, or Hoko Po, is a fearsome child-eating monster in a Taiwanese folktale. The story depicts an old tiger that had to eat three children to accomplish her dream of becoming a human being. Auntie Tigress is also a character in a bedtime song, which reminds Taiwanese children that Auntie Tigress will come to eat them if them do not sleep tight.

Butterfly orchids

Butterfly orchid, also known as Phalaenopsis, is an elegant regal flower. It is considered to be the ultimate expression of good taste and it is seen as the Empress of Orchids by Taiwanese because of its delicate tiara-like crown. Taiwan is famous for its cultivation of butterfly orchids and has been the top orchid exporting country.

Dragon Boat Festival

The Dragon Boat Festival, also called Double Fifth Festival, is a significant holiday when festivities are held to prevent evils and diseases for the rest of the year in Taiwan. It is celebrated on the fifth day of the fifth moon of the lunar calendar. Traditional customs including dragon boat racing and eating rice dumplings.

Formosa

The name Formosa came from Portuguese in the 16th centuries, and means "Beautiful Island". Formosa, also known as Taiwan, lies to the East of mainland China, the South of Japan, and the North of Philippines.

Formosan salmon

Formosan landlocked salmon are one of the national treasures in Taiwan because it is one of the rarest fish in the world. Formosan salmon are now at high risk for extinction and are protected in their native habitat in the central part of Taiwan.

Mazu Goddess

Mazu, also spelt Matsu, is widely worshipped as the goddess of the sea and the protector of fishermen and sailors in the southeastern coastal regions of East and Southeast Asia. She is also an important deity and is called the patron saint of Taiwan.

Taipei 101 (The candy house in the story)

Taipei 101, formerly known as the Taipei World Financial Center, is a landmark skyscraper in Taipei, Taiwan. The building was the world's tallest building from 2004 to 2010.

The King of Hell

It is believed that the King of Hell, also know as the Ten Courts of Hell, opened the gate of hell to allow ghosts to visit the living world during the Ghost Month in Taiwan. This is a traditional Buddhist belief across Chinese society.

Monster Nian

Legend has it that in ancient times, a monster called "Nian" (year) would come out to eat people and animals on the eve of every Spring Festival, also known as Chinese New Year or Lunar New Year. The customs is for every household to let off firecrackers, light candles, and stay up the whole night to avoid being attacked by Monster Nian.

Sun Moon Lake

Sun Moon Lake, also known as Lake Candidus, is the largest lake and one of the most famous tourist attractions in Taiwan. The lake is famous for its clear, sparkling blue water, and is set against a picturesque mountain backdrop. It has also been a center of aboriginal life, the Thao tribe, for thousands of years.

Two-Tooth Man

Two-Tooth Man is one of the most popular characters in glove puppetry, which is a contemporarily puppetry performance in Taiwan. Two-Tooth Man plays a comedy role in the show. The distinguishing feature of Two-Tooth Man is his two big buckteeth. Every puppy in the puppetry has a specific literary idiom to represent the character's personality. Two-Tooth Man's favorite and most well known idiom is: "Red flowers lack fragrance, fragrant flowers lack color, tree peony flowers radiate with both color and fragrance; smelly farts are quiet, loud farts are not smelly, yam farts are both loud and smelly". This idiom shows how random, spontaneous, and hilarious Two-Tooth Man is.

Water Ghost

According to local folk traditions, people, especially children, must avoid swimming or playing beside water such as at beaches or beside rivers during the Ghost Month in Taiwan. People believe that during the Ghost Month, there will be water ghosts looking for children to take their place.

About the Author

Author:
Ying Syuan Huang was born in Taiwan in 1988. She received her education in Taiwan, and later in Canada. She created this children's book when she was doing her undergraduate degree in software engineering. She is now a graduate student in the Faculty of Education at McGill University.

Written by Ying Syuan Huang
Illustrated by Ying Syuan Huang
Created and designed by Ying Syuan Huang

Afterword

It took me several years to finally publish this children book because of a fear that it would not being good enough, a fear of unexpected feedback, and a fear of myself as a children's book author. But Formosa inspired me to overcome my fears and begin my own adventure. Woohoo! This adventure has been so exciting!!!

I started creating this book when I was working with a child named Austin, who was diagnosed with Attention deficit hyperactivity disorder (ADHD). I was his one-on-one English tutor in Taiwan. The first time I met Austin, he was crying in the middle of the register center of the elementary school. He was alone and other students were giggling at him. My colleague told me that there was nothing to worry about because it happened regularly. Ten minutes later, Austin's mother came to him, and asked him, in front of his peers, to take his medicine. When I saw Austin close his eyes and cry even louder when he saw his mother running to him, I realized that hi was a smart child — he knew how to catch his mother's attention.

As Austin turned and then walked happily to his class, I was still confused about what had just happened. The principal came and whispered into my ear, "Just remember never to let Austin go to a class without taking medicine."

A few weeks later, the principal asked if I was willing to be Austin's one-on-one English tutor because he could not get along with other children and he interrupted the class all the time. I hesitated, but my instinct told me to take the job. From previous experience, I knew that Austin wanted attention.

At the beginning of our first class, Austin stared at my clothes and started to name all the colors he saw. We spent the whole class that day talking about the colors he liked, the places he had been, the things he did with his mom, the cartoons he watched, and the stories he liked. After class, Austin went out of the classroom and told his mother that he had a wonderful class because there was no writing, no reading, and no learning. It shocked me because I did not feel the same way. Instead, I felt that we had learnt a lot because all of our conversations were in English (in that school, not many children in grade two could do that. Most of them lacked the confidence to engage conversations fully in English). Austin also learnt a lot of English words from the class. Since then, I came to believe that there are so many ways to provide children with opportunities for learning. I decided to keep a record of Austin's stories (e.g., his trips, his favorite bedtime stories, and his memories with his mother). All of them played in my mind and inspired me to complete this book.

During the creating process, I have always imaged how Austin and his mother would be reading this book and sharing ideas together. My desire was to create a book that would make Austin

feel loved, just like when he saw his mother running to him;

feel heard, just like when he had my attentions to his stories;

and feel free, just like when he learnt without knowing that he was learning.

Printed in the United States
By Bookmasters